# Privacy

## FOUNDATIONS *of* DEMOCRACY

### AUTHORITY / PRIVACY / RESPONSIBILITY / JUSTICE

Center for Civic Education

5145 Douglas Fir Road, Calabasas, CA 91302

818.591.9321    www.civiced.org

**Charles N. Quigley**
Executive Director
Center for Civic Education

© 1997 Center for Civic Education
10 09 08    08 09 10

The first edition of this text was developed with the support of a grant from the National Endowment for the Humanities.

This new and revised edition has been prepared under Grant #95-JS-FX-0023 from the Office of Juvenile Justice and Delinquency Prevention, Office of Justice Programs, U.S. Department of Justice.

Points of view or opinions in this document are those of the author and do not necessarily represent the official position or policies of the U.S. Department of Justice.

ISBN 10    0–89818–160–7
ISBN 13    978–0–89818–160–9

# Table of Contents

Introduction 3

Unit One: **What Is Privacy?** 5

Lesson 1 What Is Privacy? 6

Lesson 2 What Kinds of Things Do People Want to Keep Private?
How Do They Keep Things Private? 13

Unit Two: **What Might Explain Differences in Privacy Behavior?** 19

Lesson 3 Why Might People's Privacy Behavior Differ? 20

Lesson 4 How Does Culture Affect People's Ideas about Privacy? 28

Unit Three: **What Are Possible Consequences of Privacy?** 35

Lesson 5 What Are the Benefits and Costs of Privacy? 36

Lesson 6 How Can We Weigh the Benefits and Costs of Privacy? 45

Lesson 7 How Would You Evaluate the Benefits and Costs
of Privacy in This Situation? 51

Unit Four: **What Should Be the Scope and Limits of Privacy?** 57

Lesson 8 When Should the Right to Privacy Be Protected? 58

Lesson 9 What Ideas Are Useful in Solving Problems of Privacy? 70

Lesson 10 How Would You Decide This Problem of Privacy? 77

**Glossary** 83

# Introduction...

Have you ever told your best friend a secret? Do you have some things in a box or drawer because they are special and you do not want anyone else to disturb them? Has there been a time when you felt a need to be alone?

This book is about privacy. You will learn what privacy means and how people differ in what they wish to keep private. People also differ in the ways they behave to keep things private.

Privacy is so important to individuals and to our free society that we often say we have "a right to privacy." Privacy also has its costs. Sometimes we have to decide when other values and interests are more important than privacy.

How can you decide whether something should be kept private? Sometimes it is easy to decide. For example, most people would agree that we all should have the right to keep our thoughts and feelings private if we wish to.

At other times, deciding whether something should be kept private can be very difficult. This book helps you learn how to examine and develop solutions to problems of privacy. You learn to use "intellectual tools" or tools of the mind. Intellectual tools are ideas and questions useful in examining problems and making decisions. They can help you make decisions about problems of privacy when they arise in your life.

*What examples of privacy can you identify in these pictures?*

# UNIT ONE: What Is Privacy?

What is privacy? This is an important question because privacy affects your life in many ways. There are many things that people want to keep private. There are many ways people act to keep things private.

In this unit you learn the meaning of the word "privacy." You learn what things people might want to keep private. You also learn how people might act to keep things private.

# Lesson 1

# What Is Privacy?

This lesson has a purpose...

In this lesson you learn three important ways the word "privacy" is used. You examine some situations where people do and do not have privacy.

When you finish this lesson, you should be able to explain three ways the word privacy is used and give examples of each type of privacy.

## Words to know...

behavior privacy        information privacy        observation privacy

## Ideas to learn...

## What is privacy?

How would you explain the meaning of the word privacy? Here are some ideas that might help.

- **Observation privacy**. Privacy exists when one or more people cannot be observed by others.

    ☑ When you and a friend are in a room by yourselves and no one can see or hear you, you have privacy.

**observation privacy:**
*not being seen by others when one does not want to be seen*

- **Information privacy**. Privacy exists when one or more people do not allow others to have information that they have.

    ☑ When you and a friend keep a secret from others, you have privacy.

**information privacy:**
*limiting others from knowing about certain things*

*How is this picture an example of privacy?*

● **Behavior privacy.** Privacy exists when one or more people behave as they wish without being interfered with by others.

☑ When you and friends form a secret club that others are not allowed to join, you have privacy.

*How is this picture an example of privacy?*

## Solve the problem...

### Can you find and describe examples of privacy?

This is the story of a boy named Brandon. Brandon likes to write stories and draw pictures. He is working on a story about a superhero called Marvin the Marvelous. This story helps you think about privacy. This is Chapter One of the story. You will read other parts of this story in other lessons.

When you finish Chapter One of *Marvin the Marvelous*, work with a partner to take a closer look at the story and answer the questions that follow it.

# Marvin the Marvelous
## Chapter One

Once again it is Marvin the Marvelous to the rescue. From his remote hideout he instantly senses that the Titans are in trouble. The Titans are his favorite baseball team. They are favored to win the World Series this year.

Marvin the Marvelous knows that only he, the strongest, bravest, smartest person on earth, can save the Titans. Like a powerful bolt of lightning, Marvin flies to his dangerous mission. He soars high above the clouds. His super vision spots the troubled airplane carrying the Titan team.

Marvin reaches out with his mighty arm of steel and steadies the tumbling plane. Carefully, he guides the plane toward the airport and to a safe landing.

The fans let out a thundering cheer as the Titans enter the stadium. Thanks to Marvin the Marvelous, the game will go on!

Marvin does not remain. He quickly returns to his secret hideout. It is the one place where he can get away from the television cameras and the news reporters. Only here can he peacefully wait for his next call to action.

"Hey Brandon, you got up early this morning. Are you writing stories and drawing pictures again? Let me see," said Lily, Brandon's sister. She was looking at his computer screen.

"It's nothing Lily. It's just. . . kind of private," Brandon answered. He reached over and turned off his computer.

*Is Brandon's behavior an example of observation, information, or behavior privacy? Why?*

"Private, in this crowded apartment? You're kidding!" Lily exclaimed. "Besides, why do you have to keep your stuff hidden? What's so secret about your pictures and stories, anyway?"

"That's my business," Brandon replied. "The stuff in my computer is mine. I'd rather not share it with anyone. Not even you."

"All right, Brandon," Lily replied in a loud, angry voice. "If that's the way you want to be. You've made your point!"

Just then, their mother entered the room. "What's the matter?" she asked.

"Oh, it's just Brandon. He's guarding his computer like it's top secret," Lily answered quickly.

"Brandon has a right to keep some things private," her mother explained. "You should try to respect each other's privacy. How would you feel if Brandon asked to see your diary?"

Lily felt a little embarrassed. Their mother steered them both toward the kitchen where their father was cooking breakfast.

Dad greeted them with a cheerful, "Good morning." Just then the telephone rang. "I'll get it," he said. "I wonder who's calling this early."

"Hello. Yes, this is he," Brandon heard his father say into the receiver. "I've won a prize? That's great! What is it?"

Brandon's father began to look angry. "You want my credit card number? What for?" he demanded. "I'm sorry, but I don't give that information to anyone over the telephone. Good-bye."

"There's little privacy left anymore," Brandon's father said, hanging up the receiver.

*Is the father's behavior an example of observation, information, or behavior privacy? Why?*

"By the way, children," their mother said, "Grandma Murphy is coming to live with us for a few months. Her house is being repaired."

Brandon wasn't too happy. "Four's too many for this apartment as it is. Now it's going to be five," he complained.

"Lily, Grandma can stay with you in your room," her mother explained.

*Is Grandma's behavior an example of observation, information, or behavior privacy? Why?*

"Mom, when Grandma visits she locks herself in my room. I think she pretends she is an important writer. I always find papers all over my room," Lily complained.

Brandon headed for the door. "I have to get to school," he said as he was leaving. "I promised Ms. Goldberg I'd come early to help her draw pictures for the bulletin board."

## Take a closer look

**?** Who wanted to keep something private?

**?** What did they want to keep private?

**?** From whom did they want to keep it private?

**?** Why did they want to keep it private?

**?** Which examples of privacy in the story illustrate

- observation privacy

- information privacy

- behavior privacy

## Can you identify the issues of privacy?

Read the following situations. Then, work with a partner to answer the "Apply your skills" questions.

*1* Raul and Miguel share a bedroom. Each boy has a desk for his personal belongings. The boys agreed not to look in each other's desk drawers without permission.

*2* Sarah got a telephone call from Leticia, her best friend. When the telephone rang, she closed the door to her room. She did not want her older brother to hear her conversation.

*How is this person's behavior an example of privacy?*

*3* "How was school today?" Miranda's mother asked. "I'm upset," Miranda answered. "A girl in my class thought someone stole her pen. She searched my book bag when everyone was at recess."

*4* Randall checked the pockets of the pants he wore yesterday. He removed a note from Dori. His mother had said that she was going to do laundry today. She always checks pockets before putting things in the washer.

*How is this person's behavior an example of privacy?*

## Apply your skills

**?** Who wanted privacy in each situation?

**?** What did each person want to keep private?

**?** In each situation, from whom did he or she want to keep something private?

**?** How did each person act to try to get privacy?

**?** Which situations do you think are examples of observation, information, or behavior privacy? Why?

**?** What are some examples of privacy in your life?

## Use what you know...

**1** For one day, as you watch television or look around at school, make a list of examples of privacy you see. What do people want to keep private? How do they keep these things private? Share your list with your class.

**2** Keep a Privacy journal or notebook. Write down a list of questions that you have about privacy or a story that includes some issues about the right to privacy.

## Lesson 2

# What Kinds of Things Do People Want to Keep Private? How Do They Keep Things Private?

## This lesson has a purpose...

You learned three ways we use the word privacy. You also learned to identify situations involving privacy. In this lesson you learn about what kinds of things people want to keep private and how they keep them private.

When you finish this lesson, you should be able to explain what kinds of things people keep private. You should also be able to explain how people might act to keep them private.

## Words to know...

| | | |
|---|---|---|
| categorize | isolation | secrecy |
| confidentiality | object of privacy | |
| exclusion | patent | |

## Ideas to learn...

**object of privacy:**
*some thing someone wants to keep secret or hidden from public knowledge or view*

### What might people want to keep private?

People may wish to keep different types of things private. We call these things **objects of privacy**. The following are examples of common types of objects of privacy.

● **Communications.** People often wish to keep communications such as letters, e-mail, or telephone conversations private.

☑ Kristi always uses a secret code when she writes letters to other spies.

- **Facts about oneself or one's possessions.** People often wish to keep facts about themselves such as their thoughts, feelings, beliefs, or opinions private.

  ☑ Luke does not want his salary made public.

- **Behavior or actions.** People often wish to keep their behavior and actions private.

  ☑ Mr. Pele does not want his coworkers to know who he voted for in an election.

- **Associations.** People often wish to keep their friendships or associations with other persons or organizations private.

  ☑ Mrs. James does not want her family to know that she joined a sky-diving club.

- **Space or territory.** People often wish to keep certain space or territory private.

  ☑ Sally does not want her neighbor John to play in her yard.

## Solve the problem...

### Can you categorize objects of privacy?

categorize:
*to put into groups or classes*

Work in small groups to think of three examples of each type of object of privacy you have just studied. Use a "Types of Objects of Privacy" chart like the one on the next page. List examples from your experiences, from stories you have read or heard, or from situations you have seen on TV or movies. Be careful not to list examples that you or members of your family might want to keep private!

When your group is finished listing its examples, each group should share its work with the rest of the class.

| Types of Objects of Privacy | |
|---|---|
| Objects of Privacy | Examples |
| Communications | |
| Facts about oneself or one's possessions | |
| Behavior or actions | |
| Associations | |
| Space or territory | |

## Ideas to learn...

# How do people keep things private?

People act in different ways to keep things private.

- **Isolation.** People may isolate themselves so others cannot see or hear them.

  ☑ Brent only practices singing when everyone else has left the house.

- **Secrecy.** People may keep secrets by not allowing others access to certain objects of privacy.

  ☑ Whitney does not allow anyone to read her diary.

  ☑ Anton does not want others to know about his friends.

*What does this person want to keep private? How does he behave to keep it private?*

- **Confidentiality.** People agree not to reveal secrets to others.

  ☑ A doctor or lawyer may agree to keep information about a client secret or confidential.

● **Exclusion.** People keep their privacy by excluding others so they cannot be seen or heard.

☑ Isaac and his family do not allow others in their home, or at their table during lunch.

## Solve the problem...

### Can you identify how people keep things private?

As you read the story *Dr. Penn's Good News* think about the ways people might act to keep something private.

When you finish reading, work with a partner to answer the questions on the Chart for Identifying How People Keep Things Private. A sample chart is on page 17.

### Dr. Penn's Good News

The Health-E Company is developing a new pill that can prevent the common cold. It is a secret project.

The owners of the company think that other companies might be working on the same kind of project. They know that the first company to develop the anti-cold pill will be able to **patent** it. If the Health-E company has a patent on this medicine, no other company can make and sell it.

The Health-E company has spent a lot of money on developing this cure. To keep the secret, only a few people in the company even know about the project. These people had to promise not to tell anyone else.

*How might limiting access to the laboratory help the Health-E company keep information private?*

A guard stands outside the door to the laboratory. The guard only allows people working on the project to enter. The scientists have to show a special pass to enter.

There are other reasons that some people want privacy at the company. Dr. Sam Penn, a scientist at Health-E, is in charge of the project. He locks himself in his office to be alone with his thoughts. He says being alone helps him to think more clearly. Dr. Penn also has a lot of information about the project that he does not share with anyone else.

One day Dr. Penn made the discovery. He hurried to tell his friend, Dr. Lupe Lopez.

*How might this scientist behave to keep company information private?*

"I've found the special formula! Just take one pill everyday and you will be cold-free!" he shouted.

"Let's share the good news," Dr. Lopez suggested.

"For right now I'd like you to keep it secret," Dr. Penn said. "I want to do more tests to make sure the pill works perfectly. I would be embarrassed if we told people and the pill didn't work or, even worse, made people sick."

| Chart for Identifying How People Keep Things Private | | |
|---|---|---|
| 1. Who wants privacy? | Health-E Co. | Dr. Penn |
| 2. What objects or things does the person want to keep private? | | |
| 3. From whom does the person want to keep it private? | | |
| 4. How does the person act to keep something private? | | |

## Apply your skills

**?** Look at your answers to question #4 on the chart. Which are examples of

- isolation

- secrecy

- confidentiality

- exclusion

**?** What are some other examples of something a company or the government might want to keep private?

## Use what you know...

**1** Draw a picture or make a collage showing the different ways people keep things private.

**2** Make a list of the kinds of things you like to keep private. Next interview an adult. Find out the kinds of things he or she wants to keep private and how he or she keeps things private. Compare your list with the one of the person you interviewed. How are the lists similar? How are they different?

*What do the persons in these pictures want to keep private? How might they behave to keep them private?*

# UNIT TWO: What Might Explain Differences in Privacy Behavior?

Most people in our country and in other countries try to keep some things private. People differ, however, in what they want to keep private—the objects of privacy. They also may differ in the ways they keep things private.

In this unit you examine some of the ways people may act differently about privacy. You also discuss what might be some of the reasons for these differences.

# Lesson 3

# Why Might People's Privacy Behavior Differ?

## This lesson has a purpose...

In this lesson you learn that people may behave in different ways about privacy. You will look at some situations in which people behave differently about privacy. Then you will discuss what might be the reasons for these differences.

When you finish this lesson, you should be able to explain some differences in the ways people behave about privacy. You should also be able to explain some of the reasons for these differences.

## Words to know...

occupation
opportunity

## Solve the problem...

### Can you find the reasons that people want privacy?

Remember Brandon and his story *Marvin the Marvelous*? When we last visited Brandon, his grandmother was moving in with the family for a few months. Read Chapter Two of *Marvin the Marvelous*. Then work with a partner to take a closer look at the story and answer the questions that follow it.

# Marvin the Marvelous
## Chapter Two

After rescuing the Titans, Marvin the Marvelous rested quietly in his hideaway. Suddenly, an incredible sound broke his sleep. It shook the walls like an earthquake. Marvin knew that noise could only be from one creature. He was being invaded by the Big Snore!

The Big Snore was not an evil monster. In fact, she had a heart of gold. She was a kind and generous grandmother. Yet she snored with a roar so loud it shook every nerve in his body.

Marvin the Marvelous had a heart of gold, too. He could not ask the gentle monster to leave. She would have no place to go. After days of listening to snoring, snoring, and more snoring, he couldn't stand it another minute. He had no choice. He packed a bag and left his hideaway. In a few minutes he found a deserted hut. "Ah, at long last," he said, "peace, quiet, and privacy!"

Just then, Lily knocked on the bathroom door. "Brandon, are you in there?" she asked in an irritated voice.

Without waiting for an answer, she barged in. "Have you gone nuts, sitting in the bathtub drawing your silly pictures?"

That morning Brandon was in a very bad mood. "Listen Lily, this is supposed to be a private place," Brandon snapped.

*How does Brandon behave to keep his drawings private?*

*What do the members of Brandon's family want to keep private? How do they behave differently to keep them private?*

Lily reminded Brandon that he was in the bathroom, a place all family members had to use. She suggested that Brandon go back to his computer.

"I keep hearing Grandma snoring," he said. "The noise comes right through your bedroom wall."

By now the whole family was stirring. One by one they came in and out of the bathroom.

"Well, this is certainly a strange place," exclaimed Brandon's father.

"Goodness, this is quite a crowd of people in and out of here," declared Grandma.

"Well, I'm leaving!" Brandon said. "That finishes another great idea. I just need some time by myself, to think and to draw. That doesn't seem too much to ask."

Brandon dressed and walked out of the house. He continued to talk to himself. "I mean, Lily likes to be alone when she's talking to one of her friends. She's always saying that what they talk about is none of my business. She even whispers secrets to her silly teddy bear."

Brandon reached the park. "Sometimes Mom and Dad go out to dinner by themselves," he continued. "They say that they need a little time together without the rest of the family."

Soon Brandon came to a grove of oak trees near the edge of the park.

"Wait a minute! I know what Marvin the Marvelous did when the Big Snore invaded his hideaway. I made him escape to that little hut where he could be alone. From now on, when I want to draw in private, I'll just come here. No one is ever in this grove of oak trees even when the rest of the park is crowded."

Brandon began to smile. "From now on, I'll call this place Oak Grove Hideaway. I will be the only one who knows about it."

*How does Brandon behave to keep his drawings private?*

## Take a closer look

**?** What things did Brandon try to keep private? Why did he want to keep them private?

**?** How did Brandon behave to keep these things private?

**?** What things did other members of Brandon's family try to keep private? Why?

**?** How did each member of the family behave to keep things private?

**?** What reasons might explain the differences in the ways Brandon and members of his family differed about privacy?

## Why do people differ in their privacy behavior?

People may have different ideas about what they want to keep private. They also may differ in the ways they behave to keep things private. How can you explain these differences?

There are many reasons for people's differing ideas and behaviors toward privacy. You might have already identified some of these reasons in your discussions. Did your reasons include any of the following ideas?

**occupation:**
*a person's work or job*

- **Family.** A person's experiences while growing up might influence how he or she feels about privacy and behaves to get privacy.

  ☑ Jerry lives in a small apartment with four brothers and sisters. He has few chances to be alone. His parents teach their children that it is important to respect other people's privacy.

- **Occupation or interests.** What a person does in his or her job or hobbies might require privacy.

  ☑ Jerry is a good student. He needs to concentrate on his homework without people interfering with what he is doing. When his sisters watch him, he does not feel free to do his work.

*Why might people behave differently to keep things private?*

- **Opportunities for privacy.** How a person acts to get privacy might depend on what chances he or she has for privacy.

**opportunity:**
*a favorable time to do something*

  ☑ Jerry has few opportunities for privacy at home. There is a beach nearby where he goes when he feels the need to be alone.

- **Importance placed on privacy.** Some people think privacy is very important. Other people may think other things are more important. There is also a difference in the importance people in different countries place on privacy.

☑ In some countries, people believe that children should have separate rooms from birth. If Jerry lived in that culture he would have his own room. In other cultures, children share their parent's sleeping quarters until they reach a certain age. If Jerry lived in that culture, he and his brothers and sisters would share the sleeping area of the house with their parents.

☑ In the United States, the police are not allowed to listen to people's telephone conversations unless they have a very good reason. They also need the approval of a judge. In some other nations police can listen to phone conversations whenever they want to.

- **Individual differences among people.** Even in the same family people do not feel or act the same way about privacy.

☑ Jerry believes that he cannot work with people watching him. His sisters, Zoe and Caroline, enjoy having lots of people around. They are more outgoing and work better if they can talk about what they are doing.

Think about these reasons for the ways people feel and act about privacy as you work on the next exercise.

*How might you explain why Jerry and his sisters act differently about privacy?*

## Solve the problem...

### Can you explain why the people in these situations differ in their privacy behavior?

Read the following situations. Think about the reasons why these people act and feel as they do. Use the ideas you learned about different privacy beliefs and feelings. Work with a partner to answer the "Apply your skills" questions.

*What reasons might help explain Tomas's privacy behavior?*

**1** Karen lives in a big house with her parents and three sisters. Each girl has her own room. Karen loves to be alone to read her books. When she wants to be alone, she goes into her room and closes the door. She knows no one will bother her.

**2** Tomas has a viewphone. This is a telephone with a viewing screen attached to it. When someone calls Tomas, they can see him as well as talk to him. Sometimes he does not want them to see him or his room. When he feels this way, he flips a switch and turns off the viewing device.

**3** Bruce lives in the mountains. Every fall he hunts deer. He does not like others to disturb him. He can go for weeks without ever seeing another human being. His brother Jack never leaves the city. Jack is excited about being in crowds of people.

**4** Jane is a lawyer. When the judge asked her to give some information that her client wanted kept private, she refused to answer because of confidentiality.

*What reasons might explain Jane's privacy behavior?*

## Apply your skills

**?** What does the person in each situation want to keep private?

**?** How does the person act to keep these things private?

**?** How can you explain why each person might have behaved as he or she did about privacy?

**?** How do you explain the differences in their behavior?

## Use what you know...

**1** Draw a design for the inside of a house. Then explain to your class how living there might affect a person's privacy.

**2** Write a story about privacy in a future society. Explain what the people who live there want to keep private and how they try to get privacy. You may read your story to the class.

# Lesson 4

# How Does Culture Affect People's Ideas about Privacy?

## This lesson has a purpose...

In this lesson you examine situations of privacy in three cultures. You will read about Japan, Albania, and the Canadian Arctic.

When you finish this lesson, you should be able to give examples of how people from different cultures might feel or act about privacy. You should be able to explain how such beliefs and practices differ from your own.

## Words to know...

| | | |
|---|---|---|
| culture | Inuit | solitude |
| Gypsy | shaman | |

## Ideas to learn...

**culture:**
*the customs, beliefs, laws, way of living, and all other results of human work and thought that belong to people*

### What are cultural ideas about privacy?

Privacy is found in all **cultures** of the world. Individuals might have different opinions about what they want to keep private. They also might differ in the ways they keep things private.

How people feel about privacy and act to get privacy might differ among cultures. It is interesting to compare the privacy behavior of people in various cultures to see how they are the same and how they are different. It is also interesting to try to understand why people of various cultures feel and act in certain ways towards privacy.

## Solve the problem...

# Can you explain the similarities and differences in the ways people behave about privacy in these stories?

This exercise includes stories about privacy in different cultures. Work in groups of three students. Each student in the group should read a different story. After each person reads the story, he or she should complete the "Chart for Identifying How People Keep Things Private." A sample chart is on page 34. Then each student should share his or her story with the group.

## Story # 1

The idea of having private space in Japan is not traditional. It is a new idea that comes from the fact that many customs in the East and West are now being shared. The word used for privacy in Japan is the English word but it is pronounced in Japanese fashion.

### A Visit to Tokyo

My name is Hirota and my twin brother is Kishi. We are twelve years old. We live with our parents in an apartment building in Tokyo. Our apartment has three rooms.

The main room for entertaining guests becomes a bedroom at night. Futons are laid out on the floor for our parents. We have our own room.

Everyday we walk to and from school by ourselves. We feel safe because of the *koban* in our neighborhood.

Kobans are small police stations where one or two police officers work at a time. One koban is responsible for about 300 households and businesses. All the officers know us. If we did not come home on time the officers would alert our mother or father at work.

*How do people in your culture differ from the Japanese in their feelings toward the police and privacy? How are their feelings similar?*

**Page 29**

The officers spend several hours a day visiting and talking to the families and businesses on their beat. They do this at every home and business in the neighborhood about twice a year.

Officers drop in for tea and during the visit they record details of the family members and their guests and visitors. There is no law that says you are required to answer the officers' questions, but almost everyone does.

Each koban is well informed about its neighborhood. The officers keep lists of old people living alone, people with criminal records, and people with mental illness. They also keep lists of people who work the night shift just in case they witness a crime.

Sometimes a neighbor will tell the police that someone has had a sudden change in lifestyle—they are driving a new car and have a television and a computer that they didn't have before, for example. The officer can file a report with the main station if he thinks it is necessary. Then senior officers can decide to send detectives to conduct a secret investigation.

Our family and friends find the police presence reassuring. We lose some privacy, but we have peace of mind.

Policing of this kind works very well in the older districts of the cities and in rural areas. But we have some friends that live in a new apartment complex that covers three streets. The police say that the people who live in these kinds of complexes are less cooperative. They are less likely to form neighborhood crime prevention organizations. They also have a greater desire for privacy. My brother and I think this is because they live so close to each other.

**Gypsy:**
*a member of a wandering group of people who come from India to Europe in the fourteenth and fifteenth centuries and now live in many parts of the world*

## Story #2

This story is about the **Gypsies** of Eastern Europe. The people in our story live in Albania. The Gypsy people call themselves Rom and they speak Romany.

# A Visit to Albania

My name is Lena. I am Rom and I live with my family in a small village in Albania. Last summer we had a guest from the United States. Within a day the whole neighborhood knew Margaret was here and that she was visiting our family.

Margaret was not allowed to go out alone. This was partly because she's a woman and partly because she was a guest. Sometimes she tried to slip out to go for a walk alone. But my big brother Nico, or someone else, would quickly appear at her side.

Even in the house we did not allow her to be alone. Our family does not need privacy or quiet. The more people around, and the noisier they are, the better we like it. This is our way.

*How do people in your culture differ from the Rom in their feelings about people who want to be alone? How are their feelings similar?*

We believe that there must be something wrong with you, if you want to be alone.

Of course, in the morning it's different. All the women ignore all the men for a time, and the men ignore the women also. Nobody speaks to a man in the morning before he washes himself. We know not to see someone who is not yet ready to be seen. It is easy to pretend there are walls between us.

Branko is the oldest in the family. He has been saving money to buy an apartment for himself and his wife. The money is hidden. Everyone knows about it, but we don't talk about it.

One night, Branko was making noise in the kitchen. It was dark, but I tried to watch him. One by one, he lifted the pots from the stack. When he got to the bottom, he suddenly became quiet.

He placed the pot on the chair and pulled off the lid. He reached in and pulled out some bundles. It was the money for the apartment. Each bundle was tied with a string. He lowered six bundles into a laundry bag. Then he took the bag of money and slipped out the front gate.

That evening he returned with the deed for the apartment. The whole family and all our friends had a party with lots of music and dancing to celebrate.

## Story #3

The following story was collected by the Danish explorer Knud Rasmussen. During the years 1923 and 1924, he traveled across the Canadian Arctic. He studied the **Inuit** people in an effort to learn about the culture of the Far North.

# A Visit to the Northwest Territories in 1923

adapted from Knud Rasmussen's

*Observations on the Intellectual Culture of the Caribou Eskimos, pp. 52-4.*

My name is Igjugarjuk and I am a shaman. When it was time for me to become a shaman, my instructor was my uncle. He dragged me on his sled far away on the other side of where our people camped. It was in winter and there was a new moon. I was not taken home again until the next moon was of the same size.

My uncle built a small snow hut. It was only large enough for me to get into and sit down. There I was shut in. After I sat there five days, my uncle came with water.

Not until fifteen days afterwards did he come again, just giving himself time to hand the water to me, and then he was gone. Even the old shaman was not allowed to interrupt my solitude.

My uncle had told me to think of only one thing all the time I was in the hut. I should want only one single thing, he said, and that was to be a shaman. Towards the end of the thirty days a helping spirit came to me, a lovely and beautiful helping spirit. She was a sign that I would have powers and that I would be a shaman.

**Inuit:**
*a group of people who live in northern Canada, Greenland, Alaska, and eastern Siberia*

**shaman:**
*a spiritual leader who is thought to be able to cure illness and foretell events*

**solitude:**
*being alone*

When a new moon had the same size as the one that had shone for us when we left our people, my uncle came again with his little sled and pulled me home.

*How might your need for privacy be similar or different from the shaman in this story?*

For a whole year I had to have my own little cooking pot and my own meat dish. No one was allowed to eat of what had been cooked for me. Later, when I had become myself again, I understood that I had become the shaman of my village.

My neighbors or people from other villages call me to heal a sick person, or to inspect a route that they are going to travel.

When this happens, I leave my house and go out into solitude, away from the dwellings. If anything difficult has to be found out, my solitude must be for three days and two nights. I can doze and dream about what I have come out to find.

Every morning, I come home and report on what I have so far found out. As soon as I have spoken, however, I return again to places where I can be quite alone.

True wisdom is only to be found far away from people, out in the great solitude. It is not found in play but only through suffering. Solitude and suffering open the human mind and a shaman must seek his wisdom there.

| Chart for Identifying How People Keep Things Private | | | |
|---|---|---|---|
| | Japan | Albania | Canadian Arctic |
| 1. Who wants privacy? | | | |
| 2. What objects or things does the person want to keep private? | | | |
| 3. From whom does the person want to keep it private? | | | |
| 4. How does the person act to keep something private? | | | |

# Apply your skills

**?** Describe how the people in your story felt and acted about privacy. Explain why they acted the way they did about privacy.

**?** How are the beliefs, feelings, and actions about privacy in the story the same or different from yours? What would explain the similarities? What would explain the differences?

# Use what you know...

**1** Be a researcher. Ask your grandparents (or someone close to their age), your parents or guardian, and your brothers, sisters, or friends how they feel and act about privacy. Are their beliefs and feelings similar to those of the people you read about? Report your findings to the class.

**2** With a friend write a poem or song about your views on privacy.

*What are the benefits and costs of privacy in these pictures?*

# UNIT THREE: What Are Possible Consequences of Privacy?

By now you have a good idea what privacy means and how people act to get privacy. You also understand why some people might think and act differently than others when they want privacy.

In this unit you learn that privacy is helpful in some ways. On the other hand, having privacy also has some disadvantages. We call the helpful things about privacy the **benefits** of privacy. We call the disadvantages the **costs** of privacy.

It is not always easy to decide which is more important in a situation—the **benefits** or the **costs**. People might have different ideas about which is more important when they make decisions. When we make decisions about issues of privacy we usually want the benefits to outweigh the costs. Many times we have to think about how our decisions affect us and the people with whom we live and work.

In this unit, you have a chance to think about the benefits and costs of privacy for yourself and others. You learn a set of intellectual tools to help you examine and make decisions about the benefits and costs of privacy.

# Lesson 5

# What Are the Benefits and Costs of Privacy?

## This lesson has a purpose...

In this lesson you learn to identify some things that might happen when people have privacy. These are called the consequences of privacy. You learn to classify the consequences as either benefits or costs: advantages or disadvantages. You also learn some common benefits and costs of having privacy.

When you finish this lesson, you should be able to identify some consequences of having privacy. You should be able to classify those consequences as either benefits or costs. You should also be able to explain some of the common benefits and costs of privacy.

## Words to learn...

| benefits | costs | security |
| consequences | resentment | |

## Ideas to learn...

### What are some consequences of privacy?

**consequences:**
*things that happen as a result of an action or condition*

What happens when you decide you want privacy? If you decide you want to be alone or to keep a secret, you know that there will be certain **consequences**, or things that can happen.

Some of the consequences of having privacy can be benefits. A **benefit**, or advantage, is something good that happens.

**benefits:**
*things that promote well-being; advantages*

☑ When you have privacy you are free to think or do whatever you want.

☑ When you can trust someone to keep a secret, you feel secure. You know that the person will not embarrass you by revealing something you want to keep private.

On the other hand, some of the things that can happen are costs. A **cost** is a disadvantage, or something you might have to give up.

**costs:**
*losses or penalties incurred in gaining something; disadvantages*

☑ When you have privacy you might get a feeling of loneliness.

☑ When you keep yourself away from other people, you will not know what is going on.

☑ Sometimes when you keep a secret, someone might get hurt, including yourself.

☑ When you keep your homework secret, no one can give you suggestions on how to make it better.

When we think about keeping something private, we should consider the consequences of our decision.

## Solve the problem...

### Can you identify the consequences of having privacy?

Remember *Marvin the Marvelous*? The last time we visited Brandon, you learned that family members behaved in different ways when keeping something private.

In this chapter you read about some consequences of privacy.

Read Chapter Three. Then work with a partner to take a closer look at the story and answer the questions that follow it.

# Marvin the Marvelous
## Chapter Three

PRESTO! Lightning filled the sky and heavy rains poured from new clouds!

Marvin the Marvelous worked on his new invention in his new hideaway. No one bothered him. His machine to create lightning and rain wasn't going very well.

Suddenly, a visitor interrupted his work. It was none other than Paula the Powerful. To Marvin's horror, Paula started poking around his machine. She reached her hand into the opening, added some special fuel, and rearranged a few wires. Presto, lightning filled the sky and heavy rain poured from new clouds.

Marvin was overjoyed. He never would have made rain without Paula's help. Marvin learned that others can help him in his struggle to bring good to the world.

Brandon finished his last drawing of Marvin the Marvelous and Paula the Powerful working together.

"Well, that one was a struggle," he thought. "It's funny, I've never had a problem coming up with ideas. But being alone so much is making it hard for me to think of new adventures. At least working in the oak grove is more comfortable than drawing in the bathtub!"

"You can say that again, Brandon." Brandon was startled to find Grandma Murphy at his side.

"What are you doing here, Grandma?" he asked.

"Oh, I come here often, during the week mostly," Grandma replied. "I write stories, some are memories of my life. When I'm here alone, the memories come more easily. I wrote the beginning of a new story yesterday and I'd like to share it with you."

*Once I knew a boy who spent a lot of time alone. He loved having his privacy. He could draw wonderful pictures that came from deep inside him. The boy never shared his drawings with anyone. He was afraid to show the world what he felt in his heart.*

*As the days passed the boy grew lonely, and his pictures became sad and still.*

"Grandma, that story is about me. How did you know what I was feeling?" Brandon asked.

"Because we all get the same feeling sometimes. It's good to have privacy. It gives us a chance to be creative, but too much can make us lonely. Sometimes we need other people to give us ideas and make our thoughts grow," Grandma explained.

*What are some things that happened when Brandon had privacy? Which are benefits? Which are costs?*

## Take a closer look

**?** What things did people in the story want to keep private?

**?** What were some of consequences, or things that happened to people in the story because they had privacy?

**?** Which consequences are benefits? Why?

**?** Which consequences are costs? Why?

## What are some common benefits and costs of privacy?

You learned that there are consequences to having privacy. You learned that those consequences might be benefits or they might be costs. These are some of the common benefits and costs of privacy:

### Common Benefits

**Freedom.** Privacy allows you to think and act freely. When you have privacy, you may not be afraid of what others think of your ideas and actions. If there were no privacy in a country, there would be little or no freedom.

☑ When Ken closes the door to his room, he pretends to be a rock star. He strums his imaginary guitar while singing his favorite song. He does not have to worry what others think of his behavior.

☑ Ken's parents and their friends feel free to exchange ideas about their government. They talk about how they can improve it when they are in the privacy of their homes.

**Creativity.** Privacy allows you to work without interruption or without others looking over your shoulder. It helps you to be creative.

☑ Tonia is painting a picture. When no one interrupts, she finds it easier to concentrate on her ideas. When she is alone, she feels that she can create a painting that expresses her own feelings.

*How might having privacy help people be creative?*

*How might privacy help create trust among friends?*

**security:**
*the condition of being protected from harm*

**Security and trust.** Privacy can give you a sense of security. If people respect your privacy, you feel safe. You know that no one will embarrass you by repeating your personal opinions to others. You can be honest about how you feel and think.

☑ Carlos knows that he can share anything with his friend, Saul. Saul keeps their discussions confidential. Carlos feels safe sharing his ideas with Saul, even ideas that others might consider unpopular.

**Protection of ideas.** Privacy allows you to keep your ideas secret. Sometimes people who invent or create things might not want to share their ideas. Privacy allows them to protect their inventions or the things they create.

☑ Trisha developed a new way to make her computer work faster. She keeps her ideas secret because she is writing a book about them. She does not want to share her ideas before the book appears in the stores.

## Common Costs

**Loss of new ideas.** You learn new ideas and new ways of doing things by being with other people. Too much privacy also can lead to a loss of creativity.

☑ Marla's teacher asked the students to list examples of privacy in their life. When Marla worked alone, she could only think of two examples. When she worked with other students, together they created fifteen new examples.

☑ Marla liked to work alone on her grammar lessons. She knew one way to write a proper sentence. One day she worked with Lisa. She learned several creative ways to say the same thing.

**Loneliness.** Having a lot of privacy might lead to feelings of loneliness. It also might make it difficult for you to learn how to get along with other people.

**Page 41**

☑ Ahmad lives in a very large city. He likes to spend his time at home away from other people. Some days, however, he feels like he is all alone in the world.

☑ When John decided to join the Boy Scouts to make some friends, he argued with everyone. He had not learned how to share or how to compromise when making decisions.

*What are some costs of John's having privacy?*

**Misbehavior.** Privacy might prevent the discovery of people who break laws or rules.

☑ At the beginning of the school year, Shawna stole Tina's new CD player. Shawna hid it in the bottom of her desk. On the last day of school, everyone cleaned out their desks. The teacher spotted the CD player. She made Shawna return it to Tina. Then she took Shawna to the principal's office.

**Possibility of uncorrected errors.** Privacy might make it difficult to correct errors in thinking or on personal records.

☑ Mike insisted on working alone on his math problems. He could never solve the problems because he kept making the same mistake over and over.

☑ Mike applied to attend a special class, but he was turned down. He thought there must have been an error in his school records. The school would not allow Mike or his parents to see the records.

**resentment:**
*an angry or bitter feeling*

**Resentment.** Privacy might foster feelings of dislike or resentment toward others. This can happen when people are kept out of a place or out of a group.

☑ Maureen, Katy, and Elise are best friends. They whisper secrets to each other all the time. They pass notes in class. They do not let others join their group. Other students don't like the three girls very much.

*What might happen when people exclude others from their group? Which are benefits? Which are costs?*

## Solve the problem...

### Can you find the benefits and costs of privacy in these situations?

Read each of the situations below. Then work with a partner to answer the "Apply your skills" questions.

*What are some benefits and costs of having a doctor keep information about you private?*

**1** Teachers keep grade books in which they record each student's grades. Students are not allowed to look in the grade book.

**2** Luis tells his friend Ramon a secret. Ramon promises not to tell the secret to anyone.

**3** Joan is enrolled for three weeks at the Happy Days Camp. The camp has a swimming pool with a diving board. Joan is a good swimmer but she is afraid to dive. She doesn't want other students at the camp to know this. The camp counselor said she would give Joan private diving lessons.

**4** There are rules and laws to protect your right to keep some information private. Doctors and hospitals cannot give a patient's medical records to other people without the patient's permission.

## Apply your skills

**?** What are the consequences of having privacy in each situation?

**?** Which consequences are benefits?

**?** Which consequences are costs?

**?** What experiences have you had that involve some of the same benefits or costs of privacy? Be careful not to use examples that you or other people want to keep private.

## Use what you know...

**1** Interview a lawyer, judge, or law enforcement officer. Ask about their ideas on the benefits and costs of privacy. Prepare your list of questions ahead of time.

**2** Write a story or play about someone who experiences either the benefits or the costs of having privacy. Compare your work with other students in the class.

**3** Write a newspaper story about a community event such as a concert, street party, or clean-up day. List the benefits and costs of how the event will affect people's privacy.

# Lesson 6

# How Can We Weigh the Benefits and Costs of Privacy?

## This lesson has a purpose...

You learned that there are benefits and costs to having privacy. Sometimes we need to evaluate whether the benefits are more important than the costs. In this lesson you learn how to carry out such an evaluation. You also learn why people might disagree about which benefits and costs are most important.

When you finish this lesson, you should be able to evaluate some of the benefits and costs of privacy. You should be able to explain how people disagree about which benefits and costs are most important in a situation.

## Words to know...

intellectual tools
interests
values

## Ideas to learn...

### Why are the benefits and costs of privacy important?

Evaluating the benefits and costs helps us decide which consequences of privacy are most important in a situation. Evaluating the benefits and costs can help you make wise and fair decisions about privacy.

People do not always agree about which benefits and costs of privacy are most important.

Imagine there is the following rule in your school: "No one is allowed to search students' desks for any reason."

Everyone would agree that a benefit of having the rule is freedom to keep personal property like journals, books, and pens at school.

Everyone also would agree that a cost of having the rule is misbehavior. Students might hide stolen property, drugs, weapons, or other improper things in desks.

*In this situation, which are more important: the benefits or the costs of privacy? Why?*

Some people might think that the benefits of having the rule outweigh, or are more important than, its costs. Others might think that the costs outweigh the benefits.

## Solve the problem...

### Can you weigh the benefits and costs of privacy in this story?

Read *The Private Meeting*. Then work with a partner to answer the "Apply your skills" questions.

*Should class officers hold their meetings in private? Why?*

### The Private Meeting

The students in Ms. Ibanez's class elected Sally, Juan, Pat, and Eric to be class officers. They are fifth grade students at Beacon Elementary School. During a recent meeting, Sally made the following suggestions:

- the officers should meet after school

- other students in the class should not be allowed to attend the meetings

This plan would help save time because there wouldn't be so many people wanting to talk. The officers could discuss things without worrying that they might hurt someone's feelings

John thought these were good ideas. Pat and Eric were not so sure. They agreed that more privacy would make things easier for the officers. Eric said that other students in the class might not want decisions that affected them to be made in secret. The officers decided to make a list of the consequences of having private meetings. After they made their list they could decide what to do.

## Apply your skills

**?** What are the consequences of privacy in this situation?

**?** Which consequences are benefits and which are costs?

**?** If you were a class officer, which would be more important, the benefits or the costs?

**?** If you were a student that elected the class officers, which would be more important, the benefits or the costs?

**?** Why do different people see the benefits and costs of privacy in this situation differently?

## Ideas to learn...

## What questions can help us decide whether to have privacy in a certain situation?

**intellectual tools:**
*a set of ideas and questions that guide our thinking through a problem*

When we need to decide whether to have privacy, there are certain questions we can ask. We call these questions **intellectual tools,** or tools of the mind. Intellectual tools are sets of questions that guide our thinking and help us make decisions.

**values:**
*principles, standards, or qualities considered worthwhile or desirable*

**interests:**
*rights or claims; something that a person wants to give special attention to*

In earlier lessons you used certain questions to examine privacy. These questions become part of the intellectual tools for evaluating the benefits and costs of privacy. Remember to consider the importance of other **values** and **interests**, such as freedom, human dignity, and the good of society when you are making your decisions. Now, examine the chart below.

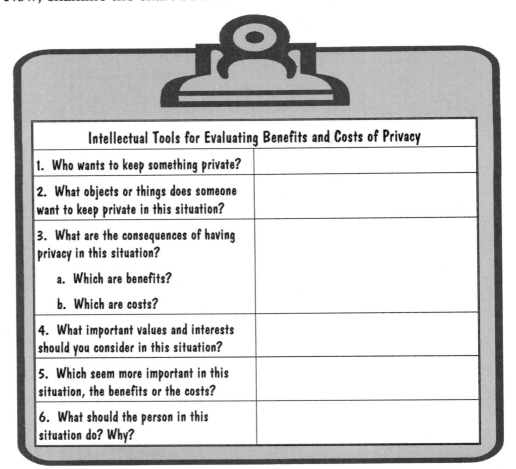

| Intellectual Tools for Evaluating Benefits and Costs of Privacy | |
| --- | --- |
| 1. Who wants to keep something private? | |
| 2. What objects or things does someone want to keep private in this situation? | |
| 3. What are the consequences of having privacy in this situation?<br><br>　a. Which are benefits?<br><br>　b. Which are costs? | |
| 4. What important values and interests should you consider in this situation? | |
| 5. Which seem more important in this situation, the benefits or the costs? | |
| 6. What should the person in this situation do? Why? | |

## Solve the problem...

## Can you evaluate the benefits and costs of privacy in this story?

Read *The Baker Street Secret Society*. Then work with a partner to complete your copy of "Intellectual Tools for Evaluating the Benefits and Costs of Privacy." A sample chart is above. See if you can help the club members make a decision.

# The Baker Street Secret Society

A few months ago, the boys and girls who live on Baker Street started a club. They decided to call themselves "The Baker Street Secret Society."

Tyrone suggested they have a clubhouse in his back yard. Everyone liked Tyrone's idea. They borrowed a large tent from Andy's family and made a sign saying "BSSS Members Only."

*Should the children change the rules of the Baker Street Secret Society? Why?*

Tyrone called the first meeting to order. The members decided on two rules for their club:

- Only kids who live on Baker Street can join the club.

- Club members cannot talk to anyone else about anything that goes on in the clubhouse.

Tyrone spends a lot of time in the clubhouse. He can talk freely. He knows the others won't share what he says with anyone else. They come up with a lot of new ideas for projects to do.

Tyrone used to spend a lot of time with Brianna but he hardly sees her anymore. Brianna does not live on Baker Street, so she can't be a member of the club. Brianna is angry because Tyrone doesn't share anything with her anymore.

Tyrone has started to wonder if the club rules are a good idea. He misses Brianna. Sometimes he feels that other members are acting stupid. They do not behave as well in the clubhouse as they do at home or at school. They talk about the same things over and over again. They come up with plans for doing things that they never do.

Tyrone finally suggested that they get rid of the rules of the club. The club members said they would decide what to do. What would you do?

*What are the benefits and costs of privacy for Tyrone?*

## Apply your skills

**?** If you were a member of the Baker Street Secret Society, which consequences of the privacy rules would be more important, the benefits or the costs?

**?** If you were Brianna, which consequences of the privacy rules would be more important, the benefits or the costs?

**?** How did the "Intellectual Tools for Evaluating Benefits and Costs of Privacy" help you decide what to do in this situation?

## Use what you know...

**1** Work with several students in your class to create a skit that shows the benefits and costs of having privacy. Perform your skit for the class. During the skit the actors should take a position on which are more important, the benefits or the costs of privacy.

**2** Watch one of your favorite televisions programs. Write examples of privacy that are shown. Make a list of some of the benefits and costs of privacy for each example. Report your findings to the class. Explain whether you think the benefits or the costs were more important.

# Lesson 7

# How Would You Evaluate the Benefits and Costs of Privacy in This Situation?

## This lesson has a purpose...

Now that you know how to classify consequences as either benefits or costs, you can put your new skills to use. In this lesson you evaluate the benefits and costs of a proposed law and weigh their importance.

When you finish this lesson, you should be able to explain the benefits and costs to citizens if the law is passed. You also should be able to explain how you used the intellectual tools to make a decision about a proposed law.

## Words to know...

| | |
|---|---|
| bill | monitor |
| state legislator | technology |

## Participating in a legislative hearing...

### Can you evaluate, take, and defend a position on how technology might affect privacy?

technology:
*the use of scientific knowledge*

Advances in **technology** raise difficult, but interesting, issues about privacy. Technology affects our privacy in numerous ways. If you use a computer at school, you might have a password to prevent others from entering your files. If you send e-mail to a friend, you might worry about someone reading your messages. Some day you might have to make decisions about issues like the ones in this story.

**monitor:**
*to keep watch over, record, or control*

First read *The Tracker Card*. Then work in small groups to participate in a legislative hearing.

## The Tracker Card

An electronics company has made a new device to **monitor** the activities of workers. Many businesses could make the device a permanent part of the workplace.

The device looks like a credit card. It has a tiny electronic chip in the center. When you enter or leave the building, you insert the card into an electronic reader.

The reader activates the card. It records your name and the time you arrived for work. You then clip the card onto your clothing. You wear the card at all times while you are at work. There are sensors in the whole building, including the cafeteria and the restrooms. The sensors track your card and send a signal to a monitor.

*What are some ways that technology might affect our privacy? Which are benefits? Which are costs?*

The monitor records where you are every minute of the work day. So, if you enter the office of another employee, the monitor knows you were there and how long you stayed. When you leave the building, you insert your card into the reader. It records what time you left work and deactivates the chip.

Many company managers claim they have a need for this system. They say they need to know what employees are doing during working hours. They need to know if their employees are following the rules. They need to check that employees do not take long breaks or lunch periods. Some companies are concerned about employee theft and drug use.

**state legislator:**
*an elected person with authority to make or change the laws of a state*

Many employees are concerned about the loss of privacy. These devices, they say, violate their human dignity. They have to stop and think each time they make a move. Employees feel like their company does not trust them. They want to maintain their privacy in the workplace.

Many employees have contacted their **state legislators**. They are asking for a **bill** to ban the use of these tracker devices.

**bill:**
*a draft of a law presented for approval to a legislature*

The proposed law says: **"Monitoring cards or chips are forbidden in the workplace."**

A committee of state legislators is holding public hearings. These hearings will be held in many cities in the state to evaluate the benefits and costs of privacy in the work place.

## People attending the legislative hearing

**Group 1 – The Legislative Committee.** You should evaluate carefully the benefits and costs of the proposed law. In this case, you want to make sure that the benefits outweigh the costs.

**Group 2 – The Employees Union.** You favor the proposed law. When managers watch workers all the time, workers feel a lack of trust. If employees cannot talk freely to one another about their work, they might not do their jobs properly. There also are times even at work when everyone needs privacy.

**Group 3 – Independent Contractors Association.** You favor the proposed law. You represent companies that do not require the devices. You do not want your employees to be monitored when they make deliveries to businesses that require the devices. Contractors say they will no longer do business with companies that use tracker cards.

**Group 4 – Company Managers.** You oppose the proposed law. You feel you need to know whether the workers you supervise are doing their jobs properly. You need to know if they are following the rules of the company.

*If you were a company owner, what might be your position on the proposed law?*

**Group 5 – Company Owners**. You oppose the proposed law. You pay people to work. You want the managers to be able to know if a worker is doing the job he or she was hired to do.

**Group 6 – Community Members for Full Employment.** You favor the proposed law. You think that the tracker devices will eventually cost many people their jobs. You think that once the owners have the devices in place they will need fewer people to supervise employees.

## Getting ready for the legislative hearing

Your teacher will divide the class into six groups. One group plays the role of the legislative committee. The other groups play the roles of citizens.

All groups should use the chart "Intellectual Tools for Evaluating Benefits and Costs of Privacy" to analyze this issue. A sample chart is on page 48.

Group 1 should select one member to act as chairperson to lead the hearing. You also should prepare questions to ask the other groups during the hearing.

The other groups should use the information in their role descriptions and on their charts to prepare a short speech for the committee. Select one person in the group to give the speech. Other students in the group should help answer the questions that committee members ask.

## Taking part in the legislative hearing

The chairperson of the legislative committee calls the hearing to order. The chairperson then calls on each group of citizens to make their presentation to the committee. Following each presentation, the chairperson gives other committee members a chance to ask questions.

*Why might groups participating in the committee hearing have different views about the proposed law?*

After the legislative committee hears all groups, the committee should discuss the proposed law. The committee members should then vote whether to send the proposed law to the state legislature for a full vote.

## Talk it over

? Do you agree with the decision of the legislative committee? Why or why not?

? Which benefits and costs of the proposed law presented during the hearing were most important? Why?

? What are some things that might happen if this law is passed by the state legislature?

? What other ways would you suggest for dealing with this issue of privacy?

? How did identifying the consequences of privacy and classifying them as benefits and costs help you make decisions about privacy in this situation?

*What limits, if any, might you place on the right of privacy shown in these illustrations?*

# UNIT FOUR: What Should Be the Scope and Limits of Privacy?

In this unit you examine situations in which people have to decide whether to respect the privacy of others. These decisions can be very difficult to make.

You learn that citizens have a right to privacy. It is an important right that Americans value. You learn that the right to privacy is not an absolute or unlimited right. There are times when our right to privacy may be limited because of things that may be more important than privacy.

This unit helps you examine and make decisions about problems involving privacy. You learn a set of intellectual tools that help you make these decisions.

# Lesson 8

# When Should the Right to Privacy Be Protected?

## This lesson has a purpose...

In this lesson you examine situations in which privacy should be protected. You also examine situations in which privacy probably should not be protected. You learn that citizens in the United States have a right to privacy, but that it is not an absolute, or unlimited, right.

When you finish this lesson, you should be able to evaluate, take, and defend positions on when you think privacy should be protected or limited.

## Words to know...

absolute                limit                scope

## Ideas to learn...

### What is the right to privacy?

During colonial times, British government officials used what were called "writs of assistance." A writ of assistance allowed any government official to search a person's home or business. Officials could enter a home or business at any time. They could search for anything. Once issued, a writ of assistance never expired.

*What rights would you have if your home was your castle? Should there be any limits on those rights? Why?*

The early colonists who came to America from England believed they had a "right to privacy." They said that a man's home is his castle. One of the things they fought for in the American Revolution was to abolish the writs of assistance.

People may gain their right to privacy by custom or law, or both. In our country it is a custom to respect other people's right to privacy by not "eavesdropping" or listening to their private conversations. If you eavesdrop, people will think you are very impolite. They may dislike you and discriminate against you.

In many situations, we have laws that protect our right to privacy. If people break these laws, they may be punished.

☑ If someone were caught looking in your window at night, they could be arrested for breaking the law and invading your privacy.

## Ideas to learn...

### Why is the right to privacy important?

*How might the experience of the American colonists affect their views about the right to privacy?*

Privacy is considered so important in the United States, that it is protected by the highest law in our land, the United States Constitution. The word "privacy" does not appear in the Constitution itself. There are, however, several parts of the Bill of Rights that indicate that the Constitution protects people's privacy from our government.

● The Third Amendment prohibits housing soldiers in private homes.

● The Fourth Amendment protects our homes and property from unreasonable searches and seizures.

● The Fifth Amendment protects us from being forced to say things against ourselves in a court of law.

The right to privacy makes many of our other freedoms work. It allows us to think and express ourselves without interference. Privacy allows us to associate with others and to worship in our own way. Privacy protects who we are as individuals. It also demands that we respect others.

*Which might be more important, a person's right to privacy or the safety of people traveling on airplanes? Why?*

**absolute:**
*without limit in any way*

The right to privacy is not an **absolute**, or unlimited, right. Sometimes other things are more important than privacy. In such situations, it is reasonable and fair to limit our right to privacy. When you enter an airport you pass through a metal detector. This tool identifies metal objects, such as guns, that might be hidden in clothing or luggage. Such objects could be dangerous on board an airplane. In this case, our right to privacy is limited to protect the safety and lives of the other people traveling on airplanes.

You should also remember that young people, such as yourself, have a limited right to privacy. Sometimes it is important that your parents, teachers, and others in authority limit your privacy in order to keep you safe from harm. As you grow older, you will gain the same privacy rights as adults.

*Solve the problem...*

## Can you identify who wants to limit someone's right to privacy in the story?

Remember *Marvin the Marvelous*? The last time we visited Brandon, you learned about consequences and benefits and costs of privacy. In Chapter Four you examine the right to privacy and how people sometimes have to decide whether to protect or limit that right.

Read Chapter Four. Then work with a partner to take a closer look at the story and answer the questions that follow it.

# Marvin the Marvelous
## Chapter Four

Brandon and his grandmother started meeting at the oak grove almost every morning before school. Brandon shared his new ideas for *Marvin the Marvelous*. Grandma Murphy had become his greatest fan.

Marvin the Marvelous and Paula the Powerful were a great team. Together they created one fantastic invention after another. One day, Marvin and Paula were working hard. They heard a terrible roar outside the hideaway.

It was the giant who lived in the castle on the hill. The giant stormed into the hideaway yelling loudly.

"What are you hiding in this hut? I want to see everything you keep in here!" the Giant exclaimed. "I'm busting into this place. Now get out of my way."

Marvin looked at Paula the Powerful. They had to do something, but what? They had to think fast.

Then Grandma interrupted, "It's terrific, Brandon. But I think you should go to school now. It's almost eight o'clock."

Brandon went to school and his grandmother walked home to watch the morning news on television:

> The city council today released a special report on the traffic and parking problems in and around town. To ease congestion on the streets, the city council proposes building a parking structure where the oak grove now stands near the edge of the park. Motorists can park their cars there and ride express buses into the central business area.

Grandma Murphy was shocked. "That's terrible. The city council will destroy the oak grove," she thought. "I've got to do something. I'll write a letter to the *Daily Gazette*. If people realize the value of the oak grove, city council members will change their minds."

Grandma Murphy's letter was short and to the point:

> Dear Editor,
>
> The City Council must be stopped. The citizens of our community need the oak grove. We need a quiet place where we can think, work, and be alone.
>
> That oak grove is very special to me and my grandson. The trees are more than 100 years old. Certainly, there must be a better way to deal with traffic problems in this city. Thank you.
>
> Yours truly,
> Mrs. Murphy

"Now, I'll take my letter to the newspaper office. I certainly hope they print it," Grandma Murphy thought.

*Which might be more important, the people's right to privacy in the oak grove or the orderly and safe movement of traffic on city streets? Why?*

Grandma Murphy gave her letter to the first person she met at the newspaper. "I'm Jane Calhoun, editor for the *Gazette*," she said. "You say in your letter that the oak grove is special. How is it special?"

"It's a private place. It's our hideaway. I go there to write and Brandon, my grandson, goes to draw his cartoons," Grandma Murphy replied.

"Cartoons—that's very interesting! If I can get some of your grandson's cartoons by one o'clock this afternoon, I'll print your letter and his drawings on the front page of tomorrow's paper," Ms. Calhoun said.

"But Brandon is in school until three o'clock. Can I bring his cartoons then?" Grandma Murphy asked.

The editor replied, "I'm sorry, but our deadline is one o'clock. Good-bye, Ms. Murphy. I hope to see you later."

Grandma Murphy was not sure what to do. She thought, "A front page story in the *Daily Gazette* would be wonderful. I'm sure it would help save the oak grove. But they'll only print my letter on the front page if I can get Brandon's cartoons by one o'clock."

Then she had an idea "Maybe I should just pick a few of his drawings myself. I know he keeps them in his trunk. They would not be hard to find."

She was still not sure. "On the other hand," she thought, "I know how much Brandon likes to keep his drawings private. He'd probably be very angry if I went into his trunk. He might not like the idea of seeing Marvin the Marvelous on the front page of the newspaper."

"Should I get his drawings myself or should I wait and miss the chance of getting the story on the front page? Oh my, I wish I knew what to do," Grandma Murphy sighed.

*If you were Grandma Murphy, would you act to limit Brandon's privacy? Why?*

## Take a closer look

? Who in the story wants privacy?

? What rights of privacy do you think they have? Why?

? Who in the story wants to limit someone's privacy? Why?

? What things would you consider in deciding whether to limit privacy in this story?

? What other ways could this situation be handled?

? What do you think Grandma Murphy should do? Why?

**scope:**
*the range of a person's ideas, thoughts, actions, or abilities*

**limit:**
*a point beyond which someone or something cannot go*

## What do we mean by the scope and limits of privacy?

You learned that citizens have a right to privacy. When we talk about the **scope** of privacy we mean the extent of privacy a person can expect in a particular situation.

You also learned that the right to privacy is not an absolute right. When we talk about **limits** we mean the boundaries of a person's right to privacy.

*What things might you consider in deciding to limit a person's privacy in this situation?*

When we think about the scope and limits of the right to privacy, we need to keep in mind other important values and interests. You learned that privacy is an important freedom. We value our right to be "let alone." We value privacy because it allows us to be creative and feel secure. It also allows us to decide what things about ourselves we will or will not share with others.

There also are important interests we need to keep in mind. We may need to prevent or discover misbehavior. We may need to find and correct errors that someone made. These interests are important to society as a whole.

*Solve the problem...*

## Can you decide the scope and limits of privacy in this situation?

Read the story *Seven Missing Dollars*. Then work with a partner to answer the questions about the scope and limits of privacy.

# Seven Missing Dollars

The students in Ms. Fisher's class were happy. Ms. Fisher allowed the children to have a lot of privacy.

Every day the students wrote in their journals. They wrote about their feelings, things that made them glad, or problems they might be having. Ms. Fisher promised not to read what the children wrote.

She also told the children they could keep things in their desks that they considered personal and private. When the students elected classroom officers, they voted by secret ballot.

One day, Sandy, a student in Ms. Fisher's class, wanted to buy a birthday present for her father. She decided to spend seven dollars on the present. That was half the money she had saved.

Before Sandy left home, she put the money in her purse. When she got to school, she talked with her friends about some things she might buy her father. Then the bell rang. Everyone went to class.

*What other values and interests might affect the right to privacy in this story?*

During the afternoon, Sandy's class went outside to play softball. Sandy put her purse on the bench. When Sandy went to bat, she hit a home run!

Back in the classroom, Sandy looked in her purse. The money was gone! She ran to Ms. Fisher and told her what had happened. Ms. Fisher asked the children if they had seen anyone take the money. No one said anything. Then Ms. Fisher told all the students to empty their pockets and purses. Some of the students said they wanted to keep the contents of their pockets or purses private.

## Apply your skills

**?** What is the **scope** of the right to privacy in this story?

**?** What might be some **limits** on privacy in this story?

**?** What values and interests are in conflict in this situation?

**?** What would you do in the situation described in this story? Why?

## Solve the problem...

### Can you solve this problem of privacy?

You learned that sometimes government officials want to limit our right to privacy. Others, such as journalists or some businesses, also might want to limit our right to privacy. Read the story *Mr. Barnes Moves to Smallville*. Then work with a partner to answer the questions that follow it. Decide what the scope and limits of privacy might be in this situation.

### Mr. Barnes Moves to Smallville

Loretta James is a reporter for the *Smallville Times*, a local newspaper. She is writing a story about people who steal from the companies for which they work.

Loretta has done a lot of research for her story. One of the people she has learned about is Harry Barnes. Ten years ago, Harry worked for a toy company in another town. A jury found Harry guilty of stealing $10,000 from the company.

*What are some things, if any, that newspapers should keep private? Why?*

*If you were a newspaper reporter, what values and interests would you consider before deciding to reveal a person's name in an article about employee theft?*

The judge sentenced Harry to three years in prison. When Harry was released, he and his family moved to Smallville. Harry and his wife both worked hard in a local factory. They saved enough money to pay back the toy company. Then they opened their own store.

A few days before Loretta's story was to run in the newspaper, Harry found out about it. A friend who works for the newspaper called Harry and told him.

Harry went to speak to the editor. Harry said the story was true. He also explained that he had paid back the stolen money. He described how happy he, his wife, and their three children were in Smallville. Harry asked the editor to remove his name from the story. Harry said if the paper did print his name, he would sue.

The editor said he would talk to Loretta James first. Then he would make a decision.

## Apply your skills

**?** Who wanted privacy in this story?

**?** What did the person want to keep private? Why?

? Who wanted to limit privacy in this story?

? How did the person want to limit privacy? Why?

? What values and interests are in conflict in this story?

? What might be some consequences if privacy is respected in this situation? Which are benefits and which are costs?

? What would you decide to do in this situation? Why?

## Use what you know...

**1** Make a list of some privacy conflicts that have happened in your school. Decide what would be a good way of handling the conflict and write a short speech to give to the class.

**2** As a class project, arrange to have someone such as a police officer, a judge, or your school principal visit your class. Ask that person to describe a conflict of privacy and the ways in which the conflict was resolved.

**3** With a small group make up a dance or mime skit that shows examples of others who might want to limit our right of privacy. Do not use words.

# Lesson 9

# What Ideas Are Useful in Solving Problems of Privacy?

## This lesson has a purpose...

In this lesson you learn some intellectual tools useful in solving problems of privacy. These tools help you examine situations in which privacy conflicts with other important rights or values. They help you develop solutions to such problems.

When you finish this lesson, you should be able to explain and use the intellectual tools in solving problems of privacy.

## Words to know...

consent                    legal right
legal duty                 moral duty

## Ideas to learn...

### What intellectual tools are useful in solving problems of privacy?

How can you solve problems when privacy and other important values or rights conflict with each other? Below are some steps that you can follow to develop reasonable and fair solutions.

**Step 1: Look at the people who want privacy.** You learned some of these questions earlier. They include: Who wants privacy? What is the object of privacy? Why do they want privacy?

**Step 2: Look at the people who want to limit privacy.** We need to know about the person who wants to limit another's privacy. These questions include: Who wants to limit privacy? How will he or she limit privacy? Why does he or she want to limit privacy?

**Step 3: Look at other considerations that can help you decide how the problem might be resolved.** There are some important things to consider in making a decision about a problem of privacy.

**consent:**
*to give permission*

- Did the person claiming privacy ever **consent** to have his or her privacy limited?

    ☑ Jackie gave the police permission to search her car.

**legal right:**
*that which is allowed by law; something voluntary under the law, such as a legal right to run for public office*

- Does the person who wants to limit privacy have a **legal right** to invade the privacy of another? Why or why not?

    ☑ Officer Garcia has a legal right to limit privacy if he sees a crime being committed, or if he has cause to believe a crime is about to be committed.

**legal duty:**
*that which is required by law; something not voluntary under the law, such as the legal duty to pay taxes*

- Does the person who wants to limit privacy have a **legal duty** *not* to invade the privacy of another? Why or why not?

    ☑ The law in some states requires doctors and nurses to keep information about their patients confidential.

**moral duty:**
*that which is required of someone by principles of right and wrong, such as a moral duty to tell the*

- Does the person who wants to limit privacy have a **moral duty** *not* to invade the privacy of another? Why or why not? We want to know if there is a responsibility based on principles of right and wrong.

    ☑ Ingrid promised Tom she would not tell his secret to anyone.

**Step 4: Look at the benefits and costs of privacy.** You learned to identify the benefits and costs of privacy. What are the consequences of respecting privacy in this situation? Which are benefits? Which are costs?

When answering these questions, you should consider some of the common benefits and costs of privacy you learned earlier:

## Common benefits:
- Freedom
- Creativity
- Security and trust
- Protection of ideas

## Common costs:
- Loss of new ideas
- Loneliness
- Misbehavior
- Possibility of uncorrected errors
- Resentment

You should also consider whether there are other ways to solve the problem. You might reject the claim to privacy or find a way to compromise. Be sure to evaluate the benefits and costs of each proposed solution.

**Step 5: Take and defend a position.** Decide what you think is the best way to resolve the problem. Explain the reasons for your decision.

Look at the sample chart on the next page. It illustrates the five steps for solving problems of privacy.

## Intellectual Tools for Solving Problems of Privacy

| | |
|---|---|
| 1. Look at the people who want privacy.<br><br>• Who wants privacy?<br><br>• What is the object of privacy?<br><br>• Why do they want privacy? | |
| 2. Look at the people who want to limit privacy.<br><br>• Who wants to limit privacy?<br><br>• How will he or she limit privacy?<br><br>• Why does he or she want to limit privacy? | |
| 3. Look at other considerations that can help you decide how the problem might be resolved.<br><br>• Did the person claiming privacy ever consent to have his or her privacy limited?<br><br>• Does the person who wants to limit privacy have a legal right to do so? Why or why not?<br><br>• Does the person wanting to limit privacy have a legal duty not to do so? Why or why not?<br><br>• Does the person wanting to limit privacy have a moral duty not to do so? Why or why not? | |
| 4. Look at the benefits and costs of privacy.<br><br>• What are the consequences of respecting privacy in this situation?<br><br>• Which are benefits?<br><br>• Which are costs?<br><br>• What are some other ways to deal with the problem? What are the benefits and costs of these? | |
| 5. Take and defend a position. How would you resolve the problem? Why? | |

## Can you develop solutions to the problem of privacy in this story?

Read the story *A Haunting Memory*. Then work with a partner to complete the chart, "Intellectual Tools for Solving Problems of Privacy." A sample chart is on page 73.

## A Haunting Memory

One evening Rodney was playing basketball on the playground. Suddenly a loud noise rang out! It was followed by the sound of a car speeding away. Rodney saw the car disappearing down the street.

*What might be some things people should consider in deciding whether to keep information confidential?*

Later, Rodney learned that Harold Williams, a member of a gang, was in County Hospital. Harold had been shot.

By the end of the week, word was out that the gang had tracked down the owner of the car. He was a leader of a rival gang from across town. Rodney knew that Harold's gang would try to get even.

Sam, a youth worker, was trying to stop gang violence. Sam came by the playground while Rodney was practicing his jump shot. "You didn't happen to see anything last week, did you?" he asked.

At first Rodney just shook his head. Then he remembered how badly Harold was hurt. Rodney just wanted to stop the violence. So, he told Sam everything he had seen. Rodney also asked Sam not to tell anyone else what he had said. Rodney said he didn't want the gang members to hurt him. Sam agreed.

Sam returned to his office later that night. Two police officers who were working on the Williams case were waiting for him. One officer said, "Sam, if there's anybody who knows what's happening, it's you."

Sam's mind started to race. Under the laws of his state he has to tell anything he knows about a crime that has been committed or that is going to be committed. But he promised Rodney that he would not tell.

Do you think Sam should tell the police what he knows?

## Apply your skills

**?** What would you decide to do in this situation? Why?

**?** How were the "Intellectual Tools for Solving Problems of Privacy" helpful in thinking about this problem?

## Ideas to learn...

### When is it better not to keep something private?

*What things should young people, such as yourself, consider in deciding whether to keep something private?*

Sometimes there are things people should not keep private, especially young people like yourself. Sometimes things happen to you or to your friends that might make you feel embarrassed if people found out.

There are times when, even if you feel embarrassed or even if you think that you might get someone in trouble, it is right to tell something private. That does not mean that it is right to tell the secrets of a friend or your family without a very good reason.

When is it better not to keep something private?

- When you know that something is wrong, you should tell someone in authority.

- When you feel uncomfortable about keeping the secret, you should tell someone in authority.

- When you have been threatened in any way, you should tell someone in authority.

## Use what you know...

**1** Write an ending to the story, *A Haunting Memory*. In your story, explain what Sam decided and some of the things that happened because of his decision.

**2** Think of a privacy conflict in your life. Use the intellectual tools you learned to look at the conflict and to find a way of solving the problem. Use the "Intellectual Tools for Solving Problems of Privacy" to decide what to do.

**3** Be a reporter and interview someone you know. Ask the person if he or she has ever had a privacy conflict. Use the chart "Intellectual Tools for Solving Problems of Privacy" to develop questions for your interview. Then write an article for a class newsletter.

# Lesson 10

# How Would You Decide This Problem of Privacy?

## This lesson has a purpose...

You have learned how to examine problems of privacy. In this lesson you apply your skills to evaluate, take, and defend a position on a problem of privacy in the schools.

When you finish this lesson, you should be able to explain how you used intellectual tools to decide a problem of privacy.

## Taking part in a courtroom hearing...

### Can you decide whether this school policy violates the students' right to privacy?

In this exercise you examine an issue of privacy in the schools. This exercise is based on a real court case. First read about what happened in the Vernonia School District. Then your teacher will give you instructions for participating in the exercise.

### Vernonia School District v. Wayne and Judy Acton

Vernonia is a small community of about 3,000 people. Most students participate in athletics. School sports are the major activity in the town.

During recent years, everyone noticed an increase in school problems. Teachers saw some students using drugs. They heard about others who also used drugs. Some students suspected of using drugs were athletes.

The school board introduced a drug education program and the use of dogs trained to sniff out drugs. These programs did not stop the problem. The school district then decided on a new policy.

The policy required all school athletes to take drug tests at the beginning of the season and at random times during the rest of season. The results of the tests were kept private. Student athletes who tested positive for drugs had to participate in a counseling program. They also had to submit to a weekly drug test.

Refusing to take the drug tests meant suspension from the team. The new policy resulted in a decline in drug-related problems at the schools.

Twelve-year-old James Acton wanted to play football at his school. When he tried out for the team, he was asked to take the drug test. His parents refused to allow him to take the test. They said there was no reason to suspect that James was using drugs. They said the test violated his right of privacy. They claimed that before officials can conduct a search they need some reason to believe the person is doing something wrong. The Actons sued in court to force the school district to end the policy.

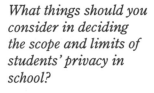

*What things should you consider in deciding the scope and limits of students' privacy in school?*

School officials claimed that since students are minors, they must expect less privacy. They said that tests were only of a small invasion of a student's privacy rights.

Only a few administrators knew the names of those who tested positive. They did not share the results of the tests with the police. They claimed that testing athletes is an effective way to deal with the drug problem in their schools.

# People attending the court hearing

**Group 1 – Judge.** You must listen to each side of the story. You ask questions that will help you better understand the arguments on each side of the case. After listening to each side, you decide whether the school policy violates James Acton's privacy rights. You should be able to explain the reasons for your decision.

**Group 2 – Attorney for the school district.** You represent the school district. You explain the school district's policy to the court. You also explain why the school district believes it is not violating the privacy rights of students. If the judge interrupts you, answer his or her questions to the best of your ability.

**Group 3 – Attorney for the Actons.** You represent James Acton and his parents. You explain to the court why James refused to take the drug test. You explain to the court why the Actons believe the school policy violates James Acton's privacy rights. If the judge interrupts you, answer his or her questions to the best of your ability.

# Getting ready for the court hearing

*What arguments might you make to support the position of the school district? To support the position of the student?*

To prepare for the hearing, your teacher will divide the class into three groups. One group will play the role of judges. The others will play the roles of attorneys for the school district and for the Actons.

Each group should review their role and the case, *Vernonia School District v. Wayne and Judy Acton.* The group should complete the chart "Intellectual Tools for Solving Problems of Privacy." A sample chart is on page 73. Use this information to prepare for the court hearing.

Judges use the information on the charts to prepare questions to ask during the hearing. The questions should help you better understand the events and people involved. The questions also should help you in making your decision.

Attorneys use the information on the charts to prepare a presentation. You should explain what happened. You should tell something about the persons involved. Finally, you should explain why the school policy is or is not an invasion of James Acton's privacy rights.

## Taking part in the court hearing

For the hearing, your teacher will divide the class into small groups of three students. Each group of three is a court. Each group has a judge, an attorney for the school district, and an attorney for the Actons.

The judge calls the hearing to order. The judge first asks the attorney for the school district to give a presentation. The judge may interrupt at any time to ask questions. During the hearing, attorneys should speak only to the judge and not to each other. This helps avoid arguments in court.

*How might a court hearing help us make fair decisions about the scope and limits of privacy in a given situation?*

The judge then asks the attorney for the Actons to make a presentation. Again, the judge may interrupt to ask questions.

The judge may permit the attorney for the school district to make a few remarks at the end of the hearing.

After listening to both sides, the judge decides if the school district's drug-testing policy violates the privacy rights of students.

Your teacher will ask each judge to explain the reasons for his or her decision.

## Talk it over

*1* Do you agree with the decisions of the judges? Why or why not?

*2* What might be some other ways to solve the problems in this case?

*3* In what way were the intellectual tools useful in examining the problem and in preparing for your court hearing?

# Glossary

**absolute** – without limit in any way

**behavior privacy** – acting as one wishes without unwanted interference from others

**benefits** – thing that promote well being; advantages

**bill** – a draft of a law presented for approval to a legislature

**categorize** – to put into groups or classes

**company** – a business

**confidentiality** – being regarded as secret; to trust someone with secret matters

**consent** – to give permission

**consequences** – things that happen as a result of an action or condition

**costs** – disadvantages; losses or penalties incurred in gaining something

**court hearing** – a formal legal proceeding in which arguments are presented by two or more sides

**culture** – the customs, beliefs, laws, way of living, and all other results of human work and thought that belong to a people

**device** – a piece of equipment made for a specific purpose

**employee** – a person who works for another person or a business for wages or a salary

**exclusion** – leave out; to keep out or shut out

**Gypsy** – a member of a wandering group of people who came from India to Europe in the fourteenth and fifteenth centuries and now live in many different parts of the world

**information privacy** – limiting others from knowing about certain things

**intellectual tools** – a set of ideas and questions that guide our thinking through a problem

**interests** – rights or claims to something; something that a person wants to give special attention to

**Inuit** – a group of people who live in northern Canada, Greenland, Alaska, and eastern Siberia

**isolation** – being set apart from others

**laboratory** – a room or building with special equipment for doing scientific tests and experiments

**legal duty** – that which is required by law; something not voluntary under the law, such as the legal duty to pay taxes

**legal right** – that which is allowed by law; something voluntary under the law, such as the legal right to run for public office

**limits** – a point beyond which someone or something cannot go

**monitor** – to keep watch over, record, or control

**moral duty** – that which is required of someone by principles of right and wrong, such as a moral duty to tell the truth

**object of privacy** – something that someone wants to keep secret or hidden from public knowledge or view

**observation privacy** – not being seen by others when one does not want to be seen

**occupation** – a person's work or job

**opportunity** – a favorable time to do something

**patent** – a government document protecting someone's invention or discovery from being copied by others without permission

**policy** – a general plan or principle that is designed to help people make decisions

**privacy** - the condition of being apart or away from others; the condition of being kept secret; secrecy

**private** – hidden from public view or knowledge; secret

**resentment** – an angry or bitter feeling

**respect** – regard or consideration

**scope** – the range of a person's ideas, thoughts, actions, or abilities

**secrecy** – being hidden from general knowledge or view

**secret** – hidden from general knowledge or view

**security** – the condition of being protected from harm

**shaman** – a spiritual leader who is thought to be able to cure illness and foretell events

**solitude** – being alone

**state legislator** – an elected person with authority to make or change the laws of a state

**technology** – the use of scientific knowledge

**values** – principles, standards, or qualities considered worthwhile or desirable

# *Photo Credits*

Page 3: FPG International/Bruce Stoddard; Page 17: FPG International/Michael Hart; Page 29: FPG International/Al Michaud; Page 30: FPG International; Page 31: AP/Wide World Photos; Page 33: FPG International; Page 37: FPG International/John Terence Turner; Page 52: FPG International/Gary Buss; Page 65: FPG International/Spencer Grant; Page 74: FPG International/Kevin Laubacher; Page 75: FPG International/Anthony Nagelmann; Page 78: FPG International/Mike Valeri; Page 80: FPG International/Ron Chapple; Special thanks: Susan Jones